THE YEAR OF
MY LIFE

一卷

THE YEAR OF MY LIFE

A Translation of Issa's
Oraga Haru

By Nobuyuki Yuasa

Second Edition

University of California Press
Berkeley, Los Angeles, London

University of California Press
Berkeley and Los Angeles, California
University of California Press, Ltd.
London, England
© 1960, 1972
by the Regents of the University of California
Second Edition, 1972
ISBN: 0-520-02328-5 (cloth)
0-520-02160-6 (paper)
Library of Congress Catalog Card Number: 60-9651
Designed by Rita Carroll

To my father and my mother

PREFACE TO THE SECOND EDITION

Ten years have passed since the publication of this book. During this period, I had occasion to translate Bashō, and the experience has led me to revise a considerable part of this book. I have corrected a few mistakes I committed in the first edition, changed my reading at several places, and added a few footnotes to facilitate understanding, but my main effort has been directed to doing greater justice to the poetry of Issa. His poems are not so simple as they often seem on the surface, and I have done my best to convey various levels of his meaning. I have also reinforced the use of colloquialism and the descriptive quality of the translation, and at the same time tried to maintain some regularity in line lengths. In preparing this revised edition, I have been aided by a number of friends, but my thanks are due especially to Mr. Philip T. Cockle and Mr. Leslie Pearsall, both instructors of Hiroshima University at one time.

> N. Y.
> October 1971

PREFACE

To bridge the Pacific mechanically is a task that today's engineers have not quite accomplished. To do the same politically is of paramount interest and importance to all people of the world. But to bridge the Pacific culturally is far more difficult than either of these, and only in recent years have attempts been made in this direction. I am not at all certain that my translation of this little book of haiku will serve this purpose, but if it should by chance bring the two coasts of the Pacific any closer together, I should be very happy.

I owe a special debt of thanks to Josephine Miles. The present work was begun at her suggestion when I was a student at the University of California under the Fulbright exchange program, and without her constant encouragement and advice, I should never have been able to finish it.

I am also greatly indebted to Seth P. Ulman, Fulbright Professor, Waseda University, Tokyo, 1956–1958. He read the manuscript several times, not only making red-pencil corrections here and there, but also rewriting sections of it. Without his assistance, the book would never have taken its present form.

My thanks are due also to Henry Nash Smith, Wayne Shumaker, Charles S. Muscatine Mark Harris, William A. White, and other teachers and friends who read the manuscript and gave valuable suggestions.

My debt to Japanese scholars and editors of Issa is too great to record here. I should like, however, to mention specially the following three books: the facsimile edition of Issa's manuscript (Haikiji Issa Shinseki Oraga Haru Kōhon) *published in 1925, which contains the Japanese characters used on the cover and frontis-piece; Seisensui Ogiwara's edition of* Oraga Haru *in the Iwanami Pocket Book Series, from which Issa's drawings have been reproduced through courtesy of the publisher; and Tsuyu Kawashima's fully annotated edition* (Oraga Haru Shinkai), *to which I owe the interpretation of difficult passages. I am also indebted to Akira Okamoto, Tadao Doi, Kaken Narusawa, Jiro Ogawa, and Michio Masui, all of Hiroshima University, for suggestions and aids.*

Finally, I want to thank the editors of the University of California Press for their cooperation.

N.Y.
Hiroshima, 1959

INTRODUCTION

Issa, whose real name was Yatarō Kobayashi, was born in the small mountain village of Kashiwabara in the province of Shinano (now called Nagano prefecture, central Japan) in 1763. He was the first son in a middle-class farm family. His father, Yagohei, is said to have had a taste for *haiku*, and left a fairly good specimen of the form behind him at the time of his death, as we shall presently see. In 1765, when Yatarō was only a little over two, his mother died. This unfortunate loss was destined to cast ever deepening shadows over the mind of the child. He testifies to the power of her memory in the following poem written in later life:

> Whenever I come
> To see the ocean,
> There is my mother's
> Beloved face.

After his mother's death, the boy was cared for by his grandmother, of whom he wrote appreciatively in later years:

She never complained of my dirty diapers, and carried me day and night on her back or in her arms. She begged milk to feed me. She borrowed medicine from the neighbors to make me well when I was sick. Since I was merely a child at the time, I was completely unaware of all that hardship, and shot up like a regular bamboo sprout.

When Yatarō was old enough, he was occasionally sent to the house of Rokuzaemon Nakamura, in the same village, to learn reading and writing. Rokuzaemon was a *haiku* poet (he wrote under the pen name of Shimpo), and it is probable that the boy received a good basic introduction to this traditional Japanese form of poetry under his tutelage.

This happy life, however, did not last long. In 1770, his father was married for the second time—to a woman named Satsu; and thus began what was to prove a long and bitter struggle between Yatarō and his stepmother. Issa has commented on his child's sense of grievance in the following passage:

> When I was ten, my second mother gave birth to a son named Senroku. Alas, from this day forth, I was compelled to take care of that baby. In spring, during the long unending evenings, my clothes were constantly soaked with his urine. Not even during the fast-fading twilight of autumn did my shirts have time to dry. If Senroku cried, I was held responsible. I was whipped a hundred times a day —a thousand times a month. Tears fell from eyes three hundred and fifty days out of the year.*

* There were three hundred and fifty-nine days in the

Above all, he must have missed his lessons at the house of Rokuzaemon, for he says:

> When spring came, I had to help my parents with the farm work. During the day, I picked herbs and cut grass and drove the horse. At night I beat straw and made shoes. Not so much as a moment could I set aside to use for study.

In 1776, when Yatarō was thirteen, his grandmother died, and he left his village and went to live in Edo (now Tokyo). No record has been preserved of his life in Edo, until 1787, when we find him studying *haiku* under the poet Chikua, at his house named Nirokuan. Chikua belonged to a literary group — known as the Katsushika Ha — interested in trying to revive the sublime style of Bashō. Here is one of Chikua's poems, entitled "Sick in Bed":

> Would I might fly
> On the back of a crane
> To view the cherry blossoms
> On the mountain.

---

year according to the old lunar calendar then in use. All the dates given in this book are to be interpreted in the light of this calendar. There is about a month's difference between the old scheme and our own. That is to say, in the lunar calendar, January begins about a month later than it does at present.

In 1790, when Chikua died, Yatarō became the master of Nirokuan, but the following year he left Edo and returned to his village. There he enjoyed a reunion with his father, and he wrote:

> On a cool evening
> Of summer,
> I see the same old tree
> Standing by the gate.

This poem marks the end of his youthful life. In 1792 or thereabouts he seems to have made up his mind to live the life of a priest-poet, for he wrote:

> For a fresh start
> At the New Year,
> I named the old Yatarō
> "A cup of tea."

Issa explains the meaning of this rather unusual pen name in the following manner:

There is a poet, who, like one possessed, runs east one day and hastens west the next day. He eats breakfast in the province of Kazusa, and seeks a night's lodging in the province of Musashi. He is as helpless as the waves that beat on the shore, and fleeting like the froth that vanishes in a moment. Thus, this poet calls himself "a cup of tea."

It should be emphasized that the particular sect of

Buddhism (Shinshū) to which he belonged was, unlike the one Bashō believed in, relatively liberal, and it was possible for Issa to be sincerely religious without sacrificing his worldly interests. The strange mixture of the sacred and the secular which we find in the pages of *The Year of My Life* can be more easily understood in the light of this consideration.

Soon after this, Issa went on a series of long journeys, and nearly all of the next ten years were spent in virtually solitary wanderings on the road. He traveled first to the south, departing from Edo in 1792, and visiting Ise, Nara, Kyōto, Osaka, and several cities on the island of Shikoku—all in the same year. In 1793, he spent some time in Kūyshū, visiting Nagasaki and Mt. Aso. When the time came to go home, he journeyed back along the same route, making many stops on the way, for he did not reach Edo again until 1795.

In 1796, he traveled again to the south, visiting Nara, Osaka, and other cities in the vicinity, and on his way home, in 1798, he stopped at his native place to see his father.

His third journey led him across the mountains of central Japan to the coast of the Sea of Japan. He left Edo in March, 1799, and returned in November the same year—but the details of his itinerary are unknown.

Issa took to the road not simply for a diversion—although normal human curiosity must surely have played a part in his wanderings. It was also a kind of poetic and philosophic discipline. For the Japanese poet, traveling has been from time immemorial a traditional way of life and of literature—a kind of symbolic and perpetual pilgrimage. It has served to keep his mind attuned to the real issues of existence, even as it has provided him with the materials of his poetry. Saigyō and Bashō afford classic examples of this tradition. Perhaps Bashō gives it the most eloquent expression:

> Days and months are travelers of eternity. So are the years that pass by. Those who steer a boat across the sea, or drive a horse over the earth till death relieves them, spend every minute of their lives traveling. There are a great number of ancients, too, who died on the road. I myself have been tempted for a long time by the cloud-moving wind —filled with a strong desire to wander.

Now it is obvious that Issa, too, is intentionally trying to follow in the footsteps of this old tradition. Notice, for example, how he begins the fourth chapter of *The Year of My Life:*

> At long last I made up my mind to travel north this year—to the northernmost part of Japan—to get more experience in writing *haiku*. No sooner had I slung my beggar's bag round my neck and flung my little bundle over my shoulder than I noticed, to my great surprise, that my shadow was the very image of Saigyō, the famous poet-priest of times gone by.

Nevertheless, though both writers may be said to conform externally to this ancient pattern of the poet, traveler, and priest, Bashō's and Issa's inner relation to the idea of travel was essentially quite different. For Bashō it was a discipline of renunciation—an exercise in solitude—and the loneliness of the road expressed the fundamental loneliness of all human life. For Issa, on the contrary, the road was a link that bound him more closely to other human beings. The solitude he experienced as a traveler only served to remind him more strongly of the happy home he had left behind. And it is characteristic of him that while on the road he should constantly be seeking a friend with whom to pass the night:

> On January 13, I went to see the poet Charai, in the village of Naniwa in Kazahaya, which is seven* miles beyond the village of Tsuchikuchi, but I was told he had died fifteen years before. The man who had succeeded Charai as the priest of Seimeiji temple did not allow me to spend even so much as a single night. I had come so many miles to see my old friend and now I did not know what to do. As I wandered helplessly on, I wrote:
>
> > Softly, softly
> > I stepped on the ground
> > But alas—everywhere
> > Water sprang up.

* Here, and throughout the book, the word "mile" denotes the Japanese mile, a distance of 2.5 American miles.

However, after a hundred steps or so, I came upon the house of the poet Goi, and there I was given a comfortable lodging. I wrote:

> Under the soft moon
> I sought
> A good gate—
> And I found one.

In brief, we may say that Bashō became a traveler in order to leave the self behind and shake off the bonds of human attachment, whereas when Issa took to the road it merely strengthened and confirmed those ties that bound him in human love to the rest of mankind.

In 1801, Issa left Edo and returned to his native village. But no sooner had he arrived than his father died. He describes the scene for us in detail in his diary:

> In the afternoon, my father's pale face became even paler, and his eyes half closed. His lips moved constantly, as if he were trying to say something. Hard, tough phlegm had collected in his throat, and his breathing became difficult. Indeed, every breath was torture for him. He became weaker and weaker, until at last, around two o'clock by the sun, he lost his vision almost completely and could no longer distinguish the members of his own family. I would have given my life to bring my father back to health again, and I asked him if there was not something he might eat or drink—but all in vain.

The only recourse that remained was to pray that some divine influence might yet rescue him or that the ancient mystery of medicine might yet effect a miracle.

> No more shall I
> Fan the flies away
> From the sleeping face
> Of my dear father?

His father is said to have left the following poem behind him at the time of his death:

> Goodbye, dear ones!
> Sit you together
> At this gate
> To enjoy fresh air.

It was his last will and testament. And in accordance with this, his father's last expressed wish, Issa determined to settle down and live in his native village. But this provoked objections from his stepmother and her son, and he was unable to carry out his intention until the year 1813.

The decade between the death of his father and his actual settlement in his village was, in many ways, the gloomiest in his life. He traveled many times between Edo and his native village, attempting to negotiate with his stepmother—but always unsuccessfully. Many of the poems from this period reflect his inner disturbance:

> In the rain,
> My heart is oppressed
> By the heavy mountains
> Of Chichibu.

> The woodpecker
> Rapping on the pillar,
> Has he come
> To summon me to death?

In 1813, however, he and his stepmother finally reached an agreement, and Issa settled in his native village in the house where he was born. In the following year, he married a woman named Kiku. He was fifty-one at the time, and Kiku was twenty-seven. Although Issa left on a short trip to Edo in 1815, his simple family life in his childhood home may be presumed to have been a happy one. At least he writes of it with affection:

> The wind gives us
> All the dry leaves
> We need
> For our household.

In 1816, his first son was born, but the baby lived barely a month. In 1818, his wife bore a little girl named Sato (meaning "wisdom"). Sato, too, lived only a short time. In a little over a year she was dead. Nevertheless, among all his children, she survived the longest (except the last daughter who was born after Issa himself had died), and it was consequently she whom her father came to know the best. Readers will find a beautiful and touching account of Sato's birth and death in *The Year of My Life*.

Oraga Haru (The Year of My Life) is primarily a record of what Issa did, felt, and heard in 1819. And we may imagine that this year was, as a matter of biographical fact, indeed one of his happiest. But Issa's intention is not purely autobiographical, and we find that his account of what purports to be a "historical" year is actually an artistic deception, and that he has woven into the fabric suggestions and experiences which come from other years and other areas of his life and mind—if indeed some of them be not pure fiction. He has, with the instinct of the real artist, shaped this year so that it may more fitly reveal the truth of him as a man than any one year, historically considered, could possibly do. He has transformed it, so to speak, from *a* year to *the* year—the year that best speaks for his entire life.

Take, for example, the poignant and haunting poem that he places at the climax of his work—the lines that he tells us he composed on the occasion of his daughter's death:

> The world of dew
> Is the world of dew,
> And yet . . .
> And yet . . .

This poem reflects his true feeling for his little girl, and we might say in all sincerity, that he *should* have written it on such provocation, and yet we know for a fact that he really wrote it to commemorate the passing of his first-born son. At that time the poem read as follows:

> I am fully convinced
> That this world is dew,
> And yet . . .
> And yet . . .

It is obviously his consideration for art which makes him violate the accident of history and place this poem, in improved form, at the most suitable moment in *The Year of My Life*. He has departed from the truth to make it truer. This book is a kind of spiritual garland that he has woven to crown his life. Or, speaking less elaborately, we may say that by means of this volume, he has turned his life into a work of art.

After 1819, Issa's life plunged into decline. A second son was born in 1820, but lived only a few months. In 1822, a third son was delivered; the mother fell ill soon after and died in May of the following year. The baby did not long survive her, but passed away in December of the same year while under a nurse's care.

In 1824, Issa took a new wife, but they lived together only a few months. In the following year he married another woman. This alliance, too, was doomed. In 1827, the house was burnt to ashes. This blow proved too much, and Issa died on November 19 of the same year, survived by his wife and unborn child.

Let us now turn to the problem of Issa's poetic form, and attempt to gauge his value and significance as an artist. There are two traditional forms of Japanese short poetry. One is *haiku*, and consists of seventeen syllables grouped according to the scheme: 5–7–5. For example:

Mikazuki ya, chi wa oboronaru, soba batake.

> New moon in the sky
> And on the earth the faintly
> White flowers of wheat.

The other is *waka*, and consists of thirty-one syllables grouped according to the sceme: 5–7–5–7–7. For example:

Yamazato wa, haru no yūgure, ki te mire ba,
Iriai no kane ni, hana zo chiri keru.

> In the evening
> Quiet of the country town
> I came to notice
> The cherry blossoms falling
> To the tolling temple bell.

Historically, *waka* is the older form by a great many years, and *haiku*, in its origin, is neither more nor less than the fragment of a *waka*. Toward the end of the

Heian period (794–1191), it became the vogue to split *waka* into two sections of seventeen (5–7–5) and fourteen (7–7) syllables respectively. Each section was given independence of thought. (Usually, indeed, each was written by a separate author.) And yet both were linked together by a process of witty association. This new two-part *waka* became known as *renga* (or "linked" poetry). During the Kamakura period (1192–1392), the *renga* was developed and expanded from a simple two-part form, with a double link, to a more complex and extended poetic chain, which might contain as many as thirty-six, fifty, or one hundred "links." In the *renga* of "multiple links," the sections were held to the old pattern of the "split *waka*," and alternated strictly between the 5–7–5 and 7–7 schemes.* Moreover, each section in the chain was linked directly with the section immediately preceding. Several authors might collaborate in turn to produce these extended sequences. In the course of time the long *renga* of "multiple" links came to be two types, and might accordingly be written in either of two distinct styles: the "high" or the "low." "High" *renga* aspired to the noble style of the older *waka*, and was at first considered more serious and important than "low" *renga*, which used a humbler—not to say vulgar

* The poem would begin with a 5–7–5 section. This was followed by a 7–7 section, which was "linked" poetically to the first. The second was followed, in turn, by a third section of 5–7–5, which was duly linked to *it*. The fourth section would again be 7–7, and link with section three. Section five was 5–7–5, etc.

—idiom. During the Muromachi period (1393–1602), however, more and more people began to write low *renga* or *haikai no renga*, and it is commonly accepted that the form known as *haiku* is merely a liberated link (5–7–5) from this old "chain." The distinguishing trait of *haikai no renga* was its deliberate and bold acceptance of idiom from everyday speech. The following example illustrates the type. Here we may see both the standard technique of "linking" and the effect of the "low" idiom:

> The hem of the long skirt of mist
> Is drizzling wet.
>
> (7–7 in the original Japanese)
>
> The lady of spring
> Must have passed water
> As she rose from a hill.
>
> (5–7–5 in the original Japanese)

In the early part of the Edo period (1603–1866), however, the poet Matsuo Bashō (1644–1694) saved *haikai no renga* from this level of forced wit and comic obscenity, and gave it new meaning and value as a form of serious literature. Bashō's achievement as critic and poetic reformer can best be considered under three heads: (1) a reconsideration of the potential value of everyday language as a poetic tool; (2) an insistence on the importance of true symbolic expression in poetry; and (3) recognition of the necessity for "unity of feeling" in poetry.

1. *The Value of Everyday Language As a Poetic Tool.*—Since *haikai no renga* began as a kind of revolt against the high style of *waka*, it is natural that it should emphasize the common and "low" elements of everyday speech. By this means it defined itself and became an independent form of art. But Bashō quickly realized that the use of common idiom *per se* would not confer aesthetic probity on the new form, and pleaded for a deeper and more essential distinction. Through his eyes we come to see that *haikai no renga* has a special realm of imagery peculiar to itself. Partly this is a matter of language. Ordinary speech has values that the elegant poetic diction of the older poetry is powerless to express. But it is also partly a matter of imagery. The humble and unpretentious images of ordinary life conceal truths that the trite ornamental pictures of conventional poetry cannot reach. For example, in the poem quoted above, the "drizzling spring rain" is a conventional figure—part of the stock in trade of the traditional poet—and can be found reiterated in literally dozens of *waka* and *renga*. Such a figure, Bashō says, has no place in the art of *haiku*.

> If you describe a green willow in the spring rain, it will be good as *renga*, but if you describe a crow

picking mudsnails in a rice field, it will be good as *haikai*.

That is to say, Bashō knew that if *haikai no renga* was to have an aesthetic value it could call its own, it must explore a new realm of imagery—peculiar to itself. But he knew at the same time that the discovery of new imagery was not sufficient. He stressed the importance of the common and the lowly, not as source of vulgar, popular appeal, but rather as a technique for seeing truly and seriously what is truly and seriously to be seen. Hence his insistence on the point of view:

> What is important is to keep your mind high in the world of true understanding and yet not to forget the value of that which is low. Seek always the truth of beauty, but always return to the world of common experience.

Or again:

> The real merit of *haikai* resides in its capacity to correct and refine the commonplace. Therefore you must not cast too trivial or too superficial a regard on the objects that you see about you. This is far more important than you realize it to be.

In brief, Bashō insists if one is to write good *haikai*, one must interpret and describe the lowly and the commonplace with high serious intent. A crow *qua* crow can hardly be said to be as beautiful as a willow in the spring rain, but granted nobility and freshness of perspective on the part of the poet, it can tell us something that the willow cannot tell. Bashō was the first to define the particular realm of imagery appropriate to the *haikai no renga,* and in so doing he gave the *haiku* independence as a serious form of literature.

2. *The Importance of True Symbolic Expression in Poetry.*—In the earliest examples of *haikai no renga,* far-fetched ideas and images are brought into a forced and unnatural conjunction—simply for the sake of wit. In the example given above, for instance, there is no essential correlation between the drizzling spring rain and the urinating lady. The latter image is arbitrarily imposed on the former. Now Bashō was extremely dissatisfied with such artificiality, and recommended that his followers see objects as they really were.

> You can learn about the pine only from the pine, or about bamboo only from bamboo. When you see an object, you must leave your subjective preoccupation with yourself; otherwise you impose yourself on the object, and do not learn. The object and yourself must become one, and from that feeling of oneness issues your poetry. However well phrased it may be, if your feeling is not natural—if the object and yourself are separate—then your poetry is not true poetry but merely your subjective counterfeit.

This statement is by no means an incitement to simple naturalism but rather a plea for true symbolic expression. The intention of the *haiku* poet is not (or should not be) simply to set the mirror up to nature, or to paint "natural" images—but to find identity in nature. The self is invited to enter into the object and to discover its objective configuration through that intimate communion. This immersion of the subject within the object is the basis of true symbolism, and it was through appeal to this principle that Bashō was able to save *haikai no renga* from being either an empty exercise in wit on the one hand, or a superficial flight into sentimentality on the other. *Sabi* (dry hardness), *shiori* (tenderness), *hosomi* (slenderness), and such other principles of composition as Bashō prescribes to his pupils may all be referred to this one essential need for "true symbolic expression," which is the very basis of *haiku*.

3. *The Necessity for "Unity of Feeling" in Poetry*.— In the early examples of *haikai no renga*, progression from one section of a poem to another depended solely on wordplay. That is to say, a certain word in the first section became the pretext for introducing a related word in the second section, and that was the sole link between the two. In the example given above, the word "skirt" in the first section introduced the word "lady" in the second section, and the word "wet" called forth the word "water." Soon, however, a more complex way of linking came to be felt necessary, and the play on words was superseded by, or rather expanded to include,

the play on ideas. That is to say that the *idea* expressed in the first section had to be commented on or developed in some way in the second. But Bashō went further even than this and laid down the principle that there should be some harmony of feeling as well—a progressively evolving essence running through the separate elements of a poem and giving it unity.

> There have been many different ways of writing the first poem of the chain. But the principle of linking has been essentially of three kinds. The kind that was practiced first was based on the play of words. The kind that became popular next was based on the play of ideas. But the kind that is practiced now is based on the harmony of what I call color, tone, scent, and grace of the poems to be linked.

Precisely what Bashō may mean by the individual terms color *(utsuri)*, tone *(hibiki)*, scent *(nioi)*, and grace *(kurai)*, is too complex a question to deal with here, but taking the cumulative sense of the passage as a whole, it is clear, I think, that the new unity he pleads for is based neither on intellect nor on wit, but is found rather in the area of emotion and sensation: it is a "harmony of feeling," a progressive evolution of feeling running through the entire poetic chain from the first link to the last. His clear and authoritative grasp of this principle enabled Bashō to attain a degree of coherence and subtlety not contemplated before his time.

These achievements constitute roughly the core of Bashō's contribution to the art of *haikai no renga*. And in just a moment we shall take up the problem of Issa's achievement, measured against the background of that contribution. There is, however, still one more thing to be discussed in connection with Bashō, and that is his creation of that particular genre of literature known as *haibun*—the category into which the present volume falls. *Haibun* is a mixed form containing both *haiku* and prose. During Bashō's lifetime, as we have already seen, the 5-7-5 form had not yet been freed from the tradition of *renga*, and the technique of linking was still of vital concern to the practicing poet. However, even in that time, so much emphasis was placed on the first section of a poetic series (which was called *hokku* during the days of Bashō and Issa, but later came to be known as *haiku*, and invariably took the 5-7-5 form) that it was sometimes detached from the sequence and enjoyed as an independent poem. Now sometimes sections of prose began to be attached to *haiku*, and thus *haibun* came into existence. This process was very similar to the growth of *uta monogatari* (poetical novels) in the beginning of the Heian Period. Many of Bashō's *haibun* were in the form of travelogues, and between the *haiku* and the prose sections in these works there existed the same kind of harmony of feeling as he required for the composition of good *renga*.

Between Bashō and Issa there is an interval of about a hundred years. But even though many poets wrote *haiku* during this century, and granted that among them we can occasionally discover such a great artist as Buson (1716–1783), on the whole we must say that this is a period of decline as far as *haiku* is concerned. Even at their best, the *haiku* of these years are but feeble imitations of Bashō, and the majority of poets show no inclination to reconcile (and redeem) their commonplace imagery with the seriousness of intention their master had advised. When Issa came on the scene, he found it his primary obligation to free himself from the dead letter of convention and to return to first principles. He found it necessary to start anew and to create afresh for himself what Bashō had already achieved in an earlier time. Issa gave birth to an individual style that was distinctly his own, but it was a style built from the same truths and the same precepts which the older poet had laid down. Perhaps a comparison will best illustrate the extent both of his individuality and of his indebtedness. It will also serve to clarify the unique nature of his contribution to the evolution of the art of *haiku*, historically considered.

As we have already seen, Bashō taught his followers to use humble and commonplace images with high and serious intent. In the following poem the image of the honeycomb hanging beneath the leaking roof of a humble cottage is certainly "low" enough to satisfy the meanest taste. Yet Bashō uses it to reveal such serious depth of feeling that our first impression is rather of the somber occasion that inspires the poem. We do not notice that it is "commonplace." That is not the aspect of the poem to which our attention is primarily directed.

> Beneath the roof,
> Drops of spring rain
> Trail slowly
> Down the honeycomb.

BASHŌ

Buson effects an even further refinement than Bashō. Although the following poem may seem, at first blush, to be created out of "lowly images," in reality each of the scenic elements employed may be found in analogous *waka* or *renga*, and are cast in conventional poetic diction.

> Drops of spring rain,
> Just enough to water
> The shells and pebbles
> On the shore.

BUSON

Now, by way of contrast, it may be averred that Issa's imagery is not only humble but markedly vulgar. He is never happier than when writing of such subjects as fleas, flies, worms, and frogs. And in the bird kingdom, the humble crow and the unassuming sparrow are his favorites.

> Don't kill! . . .
> The fly is asking you
> To spare his life
> By rubbing his hands.
>
> ISSA

> Be brave,
> Skinny frog!
> Here I am
> To back you up.
>
> ISSA

In diction, too, it is interesting to observe that Issa often employs the vernacular—which is seldom, if ever, true of Bashō or Buson. His language abounds in popular idioms and in dialectal and colloquial expressions.

> Spring rain—
> A bunch of ducklings
> Winter's leftovers
> Cry on the lake.
>
> ISSA

In this use of the vernacular, we can say that Issa revived the style of the pre-Bashō *haiku*. Indeed, Issa wrote one poem that derives directly from the *renga* on spring which we quoted earlier in this discussion.

> I am sure it was
> The lady of autumn
> Who kindly passed water
> On the maple leaves.
>
> ISSA

We must not, however, dismiss Issa's achievement as merely a return to the style of early *haiku*, for there is a marked difference between his attitude toward language and imagery and the attitudes of the poets of the pre-Bashō period. These poets indulged in vulgar language for its own sake and with intent to amuse, whereas Issa is essentially serious in spite of his colloquialism. The more humble the language and imagery, the greater—and consequently the more effective—the shock with which the poet's serious intention is communicated to us. Because of this, Issa employs the vernacular and the images of daily life more freely than Bashō—and yet he is following Bashō's principle that the poet should use the humble and the commonplace with high and serious intent.

Now, what of Bashō's second principle: that the poet should see objects as they really are and thus achieve true symbolic correlation between himself and the object. When we read Bashō's own poems, the self appears to be so deeply buried in the object that it is sometimes difficult to perceive that it is there. Take, for example, the following poem:

> In the utter silence
> Of a temple,
> A cicada's voice alone
> Penetrates the rocks.
>
> BASHŌ

It may well seem that in this poem there is no self—no "subject"—present at all, but that the poet has confined himself to depicting an "objective" natural scene. And yet the incongruity between the cicada's voice and the solidity of the rocks, together with the intensity implied by the word "penetrates," reveals powerful subjective involvement on the part of the poet. Indeed it is only through the intensity of this involvement on the part of the poet that two such disparate and unrelated elements could be brought imaginatively into such unusual and yet persuasive unity. The poet is the feeling catalyst—the subject—through which these objects are related and made one.

In Buson's poetry, this unifying self is absent, and we feel merely external excitement in the interesting collision of images.

> The huge mouth
> Of a devil, ready
> To vomit
> A red peony.
>
> BUSON

The poems of Issa reveal a much stronger preoccupation with the "self" than is true of either of these poets.

Buson had a breadth of vision which allowed the greatest possible detachment from the object. And Bashō achieved a kind of objective detachment by virtue of the completeness with which he submerged the subjective self within the natural object. But whereas Issa may be said to possess the quality of subjective involvement, he does not—as Bashō does—lose himself in nature. Bashō also becomes increasingly estranged from, Issa more and more attached to, the human. His works are full of human feelings, human empathy. The outright personifications in the following poems reveal and illustrate this "humanizing" tendency.

> "Excuse me,"
> Says a frog,
> And jumps ahead
> At the Tama River.
>
> ISSA

> Tonight, in the sky,
> Even the stars
> Seem to whisper
> To one another.
>
> ISSA

We must not, however, identify Issa's "subjectivity" with the kind of personal and extraneous intrusion of the self practiced by the poets of the pre-Bashō period. They were simply interested in the monarch of their own wit, but Issa loved the objects he saw around him, no less than himself in the object. He saw these objects always from the private angle of his personal vision, but nevertheless he saw the objects. In the poetry of Bashō, the object is in the forefront of attention, and the self is deeply buried within it. In the poetry of Issa, the self is emphatic, yet due consideration is paid to the object. This divided yet mutual love of both the object and the self enabled Issa to remain faithful to Bashō's principle of "true symbolic expression" while departing from him in style.

Finally, if we now turn our attention specifically to the large work before us, we may perceive that in designing the over-all structure of *The Year of My Life*, Issa was also true to Bashō's third principle: unity of feeling. We have already seen that Bashō referred the artistic coherence of his work to harmony of what he called color, tone, scent, and grace of the poems and prose passages which combined to make a total creation. His *haibun*, though composed of variegated materials, are all emotionally harmonious and consistent in tone. But when we come to look at Issa's *haibun*, we find he seeks much sharper contrasts than Bashō. In *The Year of My Life* there is obvious and deliberate opposition between the sacred and the secular, the comic and the tragic, the beautiful and the ugly. We also notice the use of a mixed style in which the comic and the tragic are equally present in one poem and cannot so easily be separated. But such contrasts and such mixtures in no way violate Bashō's fundamental principle. If anything, they imply a more complex and vivid harmony. Issa's mixed style brings us, by way of conflict, to that unity that is Issa just as surely as the purer and more single-toned harmonies of Bashō conduce to that peculiar essence that is his defining quality.

Another structural and unifying device in the work —and one even more obviously pertinent to the principle of "progression"—is Issa's use of the natural cycle of the seasons as the basis of his "year." In part the seasons may be thought of as a literal frame that chronologically orders the sequence of events. But they also provide a metaphysical frame that allows Issa to look obliquely through the crevices of poetic vision at the design of his entire life. The seasons are metaphor as well as fact. But, to take the factual order first, we may observe that the book begins and ends with poems on the New Year celebration. From chapter 1 to the middle of chapter 3, the spring phase dominates. From the middle of chapter 3 to the end of chapter 13, it is the summer phase that is emphatic. From chapter 14 to the middle of 17, the basic tone may still be said to be that of summer, but suggestions of other seasons force themselves in and become entangled in the web. The reason for this break in the cycle is obvious. The death of his daughter (chapter 14) comes so untimely that it destroys the natural progression of the seasons like an unexpected frost in the middle of summer. From the middle of chapter 17 to the middle of chapter 19, the autumn phase is dominant, and from the middle of chapter 19 to the end of the book, it is winter.

This is only a rough sketch of the over-all structure of the work, and there are even to this simple scheme a number of exceptions, each of which must be dealt with in its own way. But it can be said with confidence, I think, that these exceptions do not seriously jeopardize the central structure, and that for each there is a particular—a compensating—reason that justifies its existence. Chapters 8 through 11, for example, are rather out of order in seasonal suggestions and seem to be set apart from the main drift of the work. But these may be defended on the ground that they introduce the all-important stepmother theme. These chapters on the sorrow of childhood (although seemingly a distraction) are in fact a direct preparation for Chapter 12, which introduces us to the happy image of his own daughter— the emotional focal center of the work. They are the storm clouds that precede the sunshine. We see again the principle of contrast, dramatically reinforced, for chapter 12—to which all these pages lead, by opposition as it were—is one of the key chapters of the book. The winter of discontent in his own childhood may be viewed here as the emotional frame of reference within which he views the radiant—but poignantly brief—happiness of his own child's tiny destiny. The joy and the sorrow reinforce each other. They are "seasons" of another sort.

Also we may note, in a more minor way, that traces of alien seasons occasionally break in upon and disturb the strict cycle he has set up (as we have already observed in the instance of chapters 14 through 17). A memory of summer crosses his mind in winter. The image of his dead child holding a melon to her cheek haunts him in late autumn, when there are no melons. Or themes may fragment and repeat at odd or irregular times. As the "year" advances, his initial impressions are absorbed and digested into the unconscious substance of the work, whence they return to consciousness in altered form, bringing with them in their wake rich associations from the earlier part of the book. For such reasons as this, we must not be too literal and insist on the seasonal cycle in too formal or strict a way—as a rigid progression of natural phenomena. The year we experience in the book is not only a natural year—it is a year in Issa's mind. It is an archetypal cycle of experience and emotion, in which the subjective and objective weather of the physical and spiritual year are figuratively woven together into a subtle whole that illustrates Bashō's principle of symbolic expression and unity of feeling at their highest. Or, we may say, equally, the cycle of this one year stands for the cycle of his entire life. Through the action of this small wheel the revolution of the larger wheel is revealed and epitomized. And yet we must insist also that symbolic as his treatment is—that although he has taken artistic liberties with "the year" to fit it to himself—nevertheless he continues to see the year. Because he is following the archetype, he must take liberties with the aberrant individual fact, but he continues to regard the natural evolution of his "year" as an objective part of the whole.

It is hoped that this introduction may have given some small insight into Issa's life and the materials and aims of his poetry. In the final analysis, however, the distance between the poet's work and the reader must be shortened by the reader himself. I have added only a small number of footnotes to the text, for fear that they might break the coherence of the work and destroy its unity of effect. I should also observe that I have rather boldly departed from tradition in endeavoring to translate Japanese *haiku* into a four-line English form. Although a three-line form would appear superficially more accurate in feeling, I found it much too short to follow with consistency. It constrained me so severely and required what seemed to me so artificial a compression that I found it harmful. Moreover, I think the four-line form more adequately approximates the natural rhythm of English speech. Issa's *haiku* seem unaffectedly natural in Japanese. Their effect in English should be the same—so far as that is possible. I have also used rather bold and abrupt lines on occasion, so that the reader may be impelled to stop and think "between the lines" as it were. *Haiku* is a poetry of suggestion. What is explicitly said is often merely a hint that directs the mind to what has been left implicit and unsaid. In translating *renga*, incidentally, I have rendered the 5–7–5 section into four lines (as with *haiku*) and the 7–7 section into three. In *waka*, I have used a five-line form. But the number of either *renga* or *waka* in *The Year of My Life* is not large.

Issa, it should be added, quotes during the course of his work a number of poems written by his predecessors and fellow poets. In each case the name of the author appears beside his poem.

をゝ春

一茶

Preface

Bashō established the true principle of *haiku* in the years of Genroku [1688–1703]. Since then, many poets have written *haiku* in sundry styles and on sundry subjects. Indeed, everything under heaven—from the skylark singing in the air to the earthworm crawling on the dust, from the unjointed wormwood to the crooked rose—has been described by their pens. Thus, every poet has his own style and subject in line with his peculiar habit of mind, and yet I think it nothing short of a miracle that all of them have somehow kept faithfully to the path marked out by Bashō, and that all have, indeed, observed the true principle of *haiku*. Issa of Shinano is a poet who learned the secret of a perfect and yet private style. Yea, his poems would tickle even Yama the great king of hell and provoke laughter among his guardians. However, not even Issa has struck out for himself or departed from the path mentioned above. He occupies a unique position in the broad history of *haiku*. Recently Isshi, who came from the very same province as Issa, planned the publication of this book, which had been preserved at his house in manuscript form. The publication was intended as a memorial to the dead poet, and therefore no attempt at revision has been made. I, too, remember very well how I met him in Kashiwabara in the last year of his life—how we talked of sundry things, how we laughed and wept, and how we said goodbye to each other—and I think it is only by the secret and unfathomable grace of heaven that I happen to write this preface to his book.

>
> In Edo on Buddha's Death Day
> In the Fifth Year of Kaei [1852]
>
> HYŌINKYO ITSUEN

Chapter One

Once on a time there lived a priest in the temple of Fukōji in the province of Tango, and he was full devout of heart. This priest desired to celebrate the festival of the New Year with all possible joy, according to the custom. Therefore, when New Year's Eve came round, he wrote a letter and handed it to his acolyte. He gave the acolyte special instructions where he was to deliver it on the following morning, and sent him off to the main hall to spend the night. The morning of New Year's Day the acolyte rose early—at the sound of the first crow—and while shadows were still clinging in the corners, he went to the front door of the priest's lodge and knocked, as he had been instructed. The priest's voice was heard from within, inquiring who it was, and the acolyte replied he was a messenger from Amida, the Buddha of the Pure Land of the West, and that he bore a New Year's greeting. No sooner had the priest heard these words than he dashed to the door in his bare feet, and flung it wide open. He ushered the messenger into his room and seated him in the place of honor. Taking the letter from his hand, he opened it and read:

> "Forsake the world of anguish and despair,
> And hasten to the Land of the Pure.
> I shall not fail to meet thee on the way
> With a host of blessed saints."

The priest was deeply moved by the message and wept until his sleeves were soaked in tears.

This story may well strike you as being rather odd, for certainly no ordinary person would choose to greet the New Year, his sleeves wet with weeping—his eyes flowing tears that he himself had deliberately provoked. Yet, I can imagine no better way for a priest—whose primary duty is to teach the word of Buddha to his people—to celebrate the festival of New Year's Day. My own way of celebrating the first of the year is somewhat different, since the dust of the world still clings to me. Yet I am like him still in this:—I, too, forbear to use the commonplace congratulations of the season. The words "crane" and "tortoise" ring hollow on my ear, like the greetings of the begging actors.* Nor will I set the customary pine beside my door, nor sweep the dust out of my house, for I live in a tiny cottage that might be swept away at any moment by a blast from the wild north wind. I will leave all to Buddha, and though the path ahead be difficult and steep, like a snow-covered road winding through the mountains, I welcome the New Year—even as I am.

> Only
> Moderately happy
> Is my spring
> My New Year.

* On New Year's Eve poor actors went from door to door, wishing a prosperous year and accepting a small amount of money in return for the little performance they presented.

My little daughter was born just last May, but I give her a grownup's portion of *zōni* for her New Year's breakfast:

> Crawl, laugh,
> Do as you wish—
> For you are two years old
> This morning.*

On the first of January, in the Second Year of Bunsei [1819].

I have no servant to draw the first water of the New Year:

> But look! A crow comes
> In his stead
> To bathe in the water
> On New Year's Day.

A lake in spring:

> Beneath this calm
> Spring moon
> Even a turtle
> Can tell the season.

* According to the traditional Japanese belief, we become a year older at every return of New Year's Day. *Zōni*, rice cake boiled with vegetables, is the most important part of the menu for New Year's breakfast. Wakamizu, or the first water drawn on the morning of New Year's Day, is also important, for it is believed to have the magical power to maintain health and prolong life.

The spring moon
Shines Godlike
Upon a flower thief
At work on a hill.

In front of Zenkōji temple on a festival day:

A branch of willow
Gray as a gray cat
Passes for a flower
This festival day.

So famous
And so beloved
Was this cherry tree
When it was young.

With feeble steps
The old man
Totters by—
To look at flowers.

Composed on the festival day of Inari—the celebrated fox god:

Amidst all the flowers
Totally without regard—
I hear poor foxes
Raise their cries.

The second of February,
The cat and I
Burn wormwood together
In my quiet house.*

Forth
From the bush
Beautiful and bright—
A butterfly!

A distant view of Ueno hill:

Above curses,
The rich white walls
Sit at their ease
In the misty air.

* The soft fibers of the leaves of the Chinese wormwood (*Artemisia moxa*; Japanese, *mogusa*) are used as a cautery by burning the material and applying it to the skin. This is a common practice and considered a panacea for all bodily ills.

A small patch
Of green rice
Is all the ornament
My house affords.

Beneath the bright
Cherry blossoms
None are indeed
Utter strangers.

February 15—Buddha's Death Day:

In silence I lie
Like the Buddha
Aloof, though disturbed
By the flowers.

Even asleep
Buddha accepts
The money
And the flowers.

Frisking merrily
For the fun of it,
A kitten is weighed
On a scale.

Beside the Tama River:

> Strips of white cloth
> Float high in the air
> As if to heighten
> The white of the mist.*

* Many dye factories are built on the banks of large rivers, and pieces of colored cloth are often seen hung high in the air to dry.

Chapter Two

One balmy day in March a young priest named Takamaru from Myōsenji temple—a mere boy of eleven years—set out with a strapping priest named Kanryō for Araizaka to pick spring herbs and flowers. Now it happened that Takamaru slipped while crossing a bridge and fell into the waters of a raging river fed by freshets of melting snow from Mount Iizuna. Kanryō heard the boy's scream and rushed to help—but all his efforts proved in vain. At first he could see Takamaru's head rising above the water, and then a hand. But his cries grew ever fainter, till soon his voice sounded no louder than the shrilling of summer mosquitoes. Alas! The young priest disappeared in the swirling torrent, and left nothing but his image—stamped on the eyes of Kanryō. Later, the people searched up and down the river for Takamaru with lighted torches. At last they found him—wedged between two rocks. It was too late, and there was none who could bring him back to life again. Even the sleeves of those unused to weep were wet with tears when they discovered in his pocket a few blossoms of butterbur—just picked—perchance intended as a happy present for his parents, had it not been for his untimely death. They carried him home on a litter, a little past eight in the evening. His parents ran up to the body and wept bitterly, in full view of all the world.

It is true that they were priests, and used to preach indifference to life's vicissitudes. But who can blame them? It is only human that their hearts should be deeply oppressed by their unbreakable attachment for the child. This boy had been alive and fresh when he left home that morning. And now it was evening, and he lay still and dead. His body was cremated two days later. As I went to join the procession, I wrote:

> I never thought to throw
> The fresh buds of spring
> Into this smoke—
> And see it rising
> Pale into the sky.

Surely the flowers, too—no less than Takamaru's parents—must weep to be cut down and cast into the flames in the course of a single day, just as they are lifting their faces to the spring after a long winter's snow. For flowers, too, have life, and will not they, as well as we, pass to Nirvana in the end?

Silent meditation:

> A giant frog and I
> Glare at each other
> Sitting face to face
> In silence.

Moonlight shining
Upon the plum tree,
Must I, too,
Steal the blossoms?

Far above
The dark corners
Of Matsushima
Sings a skylark.

A large cat
Frisks its long tail
Teasing for fun
A butterfly.

March 7—a festival day in Hoshina village:

Beneath the blossoms
No spot of shade so small
But sports its shrine
And gets its windfall.

The soft willow
Yielding as a woman,
Invites me to pass
Through the hedge.

My stomach is
Stuffed with rice cake—
Just for digestion's sake,
I go and graft my tree.

Chapter Three

It was widely rumored that certain persons had heard celestial music coming down from heaven around two o'clock in the morning on New Year's Day. And they say it has been heard every eighth day since. Some told me in all seriousness that they actually heard the music at such and such a place and on such and such a night. Others dismissed it as simply a prank played by the wanton wind. I, for one, was inclined to take the idea seriously, but could neither accept it as completely true nor reject it as absolutely impossible. For heaven and earth are filled with strange and mysterious powers, and we have all heard of the dancing maidens and the "sweet dew" that came from above. Is it not possible that the courtiers in the halls of heaven may have been rejoicing to see the world at peace and called for music —and if we could not hear it, is it not probable that it was our sinful natures that prevented us? In any event, I found myself intrigued, and invited a group of friends to come to my humble cottage on the nineteenth day of March. We all listened intently, from early evening on, but we heard nothing until the first sunbeams touched the far end of the eastern sky. Then all at once we heard a voice—we heard music—coming from the plum tree near my window.

Only the birds
Sing such celestial music
In this sinful world
Of today.

I tidied up
My garden
To give welcome
To my bird.

On a rainy spring day
The innkeeper
Assigns even a horse
A room.

Step aside, step aside,
Little sparrows.
His lordship, Sir Horse
Is coming through.

A misty day in spring.
Not a sound,
Not a whisper is heard
Inside the great hall.

Horse after horse
A man on its back;
Behind them—
Evening larks.

At Shimabara in Kyōto:

A pliant willow
Beckons invitingly
At the door
Of a geisha house.

A rustic village
Covered with bamboo!
What luck to see
A blossoming plum!

Merrymaking by day
Moon and flower by night.
Happy, happy
New Year's tide!

Tea houses
And cherry blossoms
Flower together
Overnight.

Cherry blossoms
Are cherry blossoms
Only while we wait
Impatiently for them.

HAKUHI

To pass the time
I beat straw
Beneath the cool moon
Of summer.

April 8—Buddha's Birthday:

Person after person
Pours sweet tea
Over the Buddha newborn
This long April day.

Today
Must be a holiday
Even
For the long rain.

After sickness:

> Made of dust,
> I am as light
> As the mosquito net
> Made of paper.

> Only a drop or two—
> Scattered here and there.
> The rainy season
> Must be over.

> Alas for fun
> He lifts his fan overhead,
> The blind musician
> Of the street.

> Baby sparrows
> And bamboo sprouts
> Sport gracefully
> Together.*

---

* Traditionally, sparrows and bamboo sprouts are associated together; for example, in the family crest *(mon)* of the Dates, one of the leading families of feudal Japan.

> Two houses
> Receive their annual cleaning
> Side by side
> Now the rains are over.

On a slender bridge, suspended over a deep valley:

> On all fours
> On a vine bridge,
> I heard a cry of a cuckoo,
> Far beneath me.

> The first melon
> Of the season
> Slumbers on the breast
> Of the sleeping child.

On "Doll Street":

> The clever dolls
> Serve tea
> While I sit enjoying
> The cool evening air.*

* There is even today a Doll Street (Ningyō-chō) in Tokyo. In Issa's time there were many mechanical dolls exhibited on the street, and people came from far and near to see them.

Thank God
I am not punished yet
For lying idly here
In my mosquito net.

A few mosquitoes
Are appearing.
From now the best season
For the old!

Come flies!
Have some rice!
May you too
Enjoy a rich harvest!

A solitary shrine
Set all alone
In an infinite expanse
Of white deutzia.*

---

* The *deutzia scabra* (Japanese, *u-no-hana*) is an ornamental native shrub bearing small white flowers. It blooms in great profusion in the mountains and on the hedges surrounding country houses in April and May. Its frequent appearance in Japanese literature marks it as a favorite of poets and other writers.

A quiet life:

> Bending and stretching
> Its little length,
> A worm sounded along
> A support of my house.

A poem written in sympathy for a widow obliged to make her own living:

> Where will you go
> With your sedge hat
> When all the rice is planted
> In your village?

> Cheers!
> A glorious young bamboo
> Has sprung up
> Overnight!

> A fan slipped lightly
> Underneath the collar—
> A pair of hands
> Busy picking flowers.

The mosquito knows
That I am old.
He buzzes noisily
Right next to my ear.

At Mount Togakure:

Clear, cold water
Straight
From the mountain
Into my tub.*

Whose cottage
Can it be
Beyond this
Moss-grown spring?

A lone mosquito
Bites and bites—
Attacking me
In silence.

---

* The bathtub was placed outside the house, and water was flowing into it probably through a bamboo pipe.

Watch your head
Through the gate.
Remember you are
In summer robes.

Having no flail,
I threshed the wheat
Against the pillar
Of my house.

A poem written in sympathy for a woman peddler from Echigo:

Hot wheat harvest.
Child strapped to her back,
A woman goes round
Selling sardines.

A bamboo sprout
Picked too soon—
It would bloom in glory
But for man.*

* Japanese eat bamboo sprouts. Hence they gather them when they are still young and soft. Bamboo sprouts bear no flowers even if they are left to grow, but here Issa has given them "imaginary" flowers.

In summer
A single patch of lawn—
A spot of shade—
Becomes a shelter.

Nature takes care
That even the mountain moss
Should have flowers
Of its own.

A mosquito larva
Has ascended
To the sky, where
The new moon reigns.

At the house of my friend Dokurakubō:

Reflections
From the surrounding deutzia
Light up
My bedroom.

In this sacred temple
Even the snake
Has shed
His earthly skin.

Chapter Four

At long last I made up my mind to travel north this year—to the northernmost part of Japan—to get more experience in writing *haiku*. No sooner had I slung my beggar's bag round my neck and flung my little bundle over my shoulder than I noticed, to my great surprise, that my shadow was the very image of Saigyō, the famous poet-priest of times gone by. However, I was much ashamed when I reflected on how different was his mind from mine:—his, as white and pure as snow, and mine, as black as coal. I left my home on the sixteenth day of April, and had made my way about two or three miles along the road with the help of a stick, when I was arrested by a sudden thought: I was already near the peak of sixty, and as the moon sinks finally behind the western hills, so too my life was now in its decline. Once I had passed the northern checking station of Shirakawa, the possibility of my ever seeing home again seemed slight indeed. The voice of a rooster rang out from the roof tops; I fancied he was calling out to me to stop. And it seemed as though the gentle wind that was rippling through the growing wheat was waving to me to come back. So I finally rested my aching legs at the base of a tree, and looked back along the way that I had come. It seemed as if my village of Kashiwabara lay just beyond that hill—and just beneath that cloud. It was so hard to leave that I wrote:

> I am trying not to
> But I just can't help
> Seeing and thinking
> Of my village home.

The same thought expressed as *waka:*

> My mind harks back
> Along a trail of mist
> To my village—
> Yet there I know there grows
> No friendly flower.

> Softly—
> That it may not startle
> A butterfly—
> The gentle wind passes
> Over the young wheat.

Idleness:

> The mosquito larva
> Lies idle all day.
> So I did today,
> So will I do tomorrow.

Life is brief—desire, infinite:

> Such quantities of wind
> On the floor of a spacious
> Summer room—
> And still not quite enough!

> Every morning
> Farmers cast covetous eyes
> Over the green rice fields,
> Each partial to his own.

Something I have at the back of my mind, waiting to be expressed:

> In the village
> Where I was born,
> Even the flies
> Bite deep.

> The lotus blooms
> Here as in heaven,
> But alas it is no bigger
> Than a coin.

In the shade
Of a pine tree,
A single mat makes
A summer mansion.

A song for children:

Thrice around
Flies the dragonfly
And settles
In the summer room.

KIJŌ

The firefly darts off
And leaves its light
Behind it—
Out of breath.

An old woman
Wiped her nose
On the petals
Of a moonflower.

At his lesson
On a hot day,
A boy practiced writing
On his face.

> Hither and thither
> Dancing slowly
> A big firefly
> Swings by.

On the day I took a bath in Nyoi hot spring in the village of Tanaka, I wrote:

> It makes me feel
> Even hotter to lie here
> Looking at the mountains
> I have crossed.

> When I sat down
> To pray to Buddha,
> Mosquitoes came buzzing
> Out of his shadow.

> Fleas,
> If you must leap,
> Then leap
> On the lotus.*

* The lotus flower typifies the cycle of existence and is symbolic of the idea of death and salvation in Buddhism; Buddha is frequently represented as seated or standing on a lotus. Lotuses are commonly planted in the ponds surrounding Buddhist temples. Paper lotuses are carried at funerals. The eight-petaled lotus flower *(hachiyō)* represents the Buddhist paradise.

At this home
Where I live quietly,
Even the flies have
A small family.

My favorite cormorant
Rose to the surface
Once again—
His bill was empty.*

A cicada drones on
Forever in the pine.
Will noontide
Never come?

Thank God,
I am not punished yet
For lying idly here
In my mosquito net.

---

* Cormorant fishing is both a sport and a commercial enterprise in Japan. The long-billed sea birds are trained to dive and bring up the fish. A ring is placed around the neck of the bird—this prevents swallowing the fish—and to the ring is attached a sort of leash or rein. Cormorant fishing is usually practiced at night by the light of torches and is an interesting spectacle.

A mother cormorant
Hurried to the boat,
In answer to the cry
Of her baby bird.

Chapter Five

It was rumored abroad that an exceedingly beautiful crop of peonies had come into bloom at my friend Nabuchi's house, and that many people for miles around had come to have a look at them. Accordingly, I dropped in one day to see them for myself. The flower bed was more than fifteen feet long, and laid out beneath an elaborate canopy. It was crowded with fullblown peonies, packed in side by side—white peonies and red peonies, and peonies of purple and other colors. Among them one black and another yellow especially caught my attention because of their unusual colors. When I looked once more and scrutinized them more carefully, however, I noticed they seemed rather dry, and compared with the beautiful and healthy young peonies all around them, they looked like mere painted carcasses. They were, of course, the handiwork of my friend. He had made them out of paper and tied them under the leaves of the true peonies as a joke on his guests. His witty deception greatly tickled me. And he certainly was guilty of no wrong. He charged no one a penny for coming to see his flowers. On the contrary, he provided all who came with generous quantities of wine and tea. I could not help laughing when I thought how he had taken us in, so I wrote:

Planted under cover
Of thick leaves,
Paper scraps bloom
With peony faces.

Chapter Six

The children of this province play a strange game. They take a live frog and bury him, and they cover his grave with leaves of plantain grass, singing the following song as they work. And then they run away.

> Hey ho! The frog is dead!
> Hey ho! The frog is dead!
> Come, let us bury him,
> Come, let us bury him,
> Under plantain leaves!
> Under plantain leaves!

In *Honzō-Kōmoku*, a Chinese treatise on plants, we find that plantain grass is called "frog's skin," whereas in the dialect of this province, it is called "frog's leaf." This correspondence between the Chinese and Japanese popular names can hardly be a coincidence. There must have been some special meaning in this children's game when it was first created years ago.

> Bending over
> The frog's grave,
> A deutzia tree drops
> Pure white tears.

Frogs are reputed to have taught an ancient Chinese hermit how to fly, and here in Japan they say that frogs once fought a brave battle at Ten'nōji. But these are tales of long ago, and it would seem that today, at least, the frogs have patched up their differences with mankind and settled down to live at peace with the world. For instance, all I need do is spread my mat on the ground of a summer evening and say, "Come out, Happy! Come out, my dear!"—and out of the bush crawls a large frog and sits down with me to enjoy the cool evening air. Now there shines the soul of a true poet! I consider it the crowning glory of their race that it was a frog who was chosen judge in *Mushi Awase* (Poetry Competition of the Insects), as related by Chōshōshi.*

> Serenely poised,
> The frog sits
> And views
> The mountain.
>
> A weighty frog
> Crawled out to meet
> A lighthearted
> Nightingale.

KIKAKU

---

* Chōshōshi is a poet of the early Edo period, a friend of Teitoku. Poetry Competition *(uta awase)* was started in the Heian Period, and has remained popular ever since. In the work under discussion, Chōshōshi judged thirty waka (fifteen pairs), each on the subject of an insect.

Mute, dear frog?
Is that why
You are so bloated
With words?

       KYOKUSUI

A drop of rain!
The frog
Wiped his forehead
With his wrist.

When farmers talk
Of their rice fields,
Each is partial
To his own.

A mosquito flew
Into a woman's chamber
And was seared
In the flame.

Young boys
Dive longer
Than trained
Cormorants.

Lying at our ease,
We simply talk
Of far-off thunder
And distant rain.

In my absence
I let the lazy
Mosquito net
Hang slack.

An old woodcutter
Prayed and found
This cold stream
High on a hill.

In this world
I have found
No perfect drop of dew—
Not even on the lotus.

High on a tree
The voice of a cicada
Calls after
A running dog.

May 28—It rains on this day ever since the famous vendetta was performed.*

> I made little of
> Tora's tears falling,
> And got drenched
> To the skin.

* This is a reference to the famous vendetta of the Soga brothers. In the twelfth century Sukeyasu was murdered by Kudō Suketsune, and the murdered man's sons Tokimune and Sukenari had vowed from childhood to avenge their father's death. When the elder brother Sukenari parted from his wife Tora before setting out with his brother to kill Suketsune, her tears were so copious that ever after rain fell on that day. The brothers were successful in avenging their father's death in 1193, but both lost their own lives in the process. Their story is commemorated in poety and drama.

Chapter Seven

There once lived a physician named Nakamura in the town of Suzaka in the province of Shinano. One day, just for the fun of it, he killed a pair of snakes while they were coupling. That night he was seized by a sharp pain in the secret parts, and died. His son, Santetsu, who was a stout man with a huge mushroom-shaped thing between his legs, also became a physician. On the night of his marriage, however, he found the thing he was so proud of was utterly useless, as if it had shrunk and become soft and slender like the lamp-wick. Shame drove him to other women, but the result was always the same. In exasperation, he finally hid himself in complete isolation.

Up to the time when I became aware of this case, I had never allowed myself to take such "horror stories" seriously. I had always imagined they were the peculiar province of a certain kind of storybook, such as the *Uji Shūi Monogatari* and others of the same kind.* But considering it more deeply, it now seemed all too prob-

---

* *Uji Shū Monogatari* is a collection of popular tales compiled in the thirteenth century by an unknown editor. He has obviously drawn from various sources, especially from *Konjaku Monogatari*, a collection of similar tales compiled in the twelfth century. In the thirteenth century, popular tales were collected in many anthologies, such as *Kokon Chomon Jū* and *Jukkin Shō*.

able that it was truly the spiteful vengeance of the snakes which had undone this family and caused it so much pain.

All creatures, not excluding even fleas and lice, are endowed with life. It is just as dear to one as to another, and it is a grave sin to kill any living thing, particularly in the act of procreation.

> Hopelessly captive
> In a tub,
> The fish delight in
> Cool water.

> Fly quickly away,
> Into the mist flee!
> Bird, you are
> No longer captive.

> Sleeping like Buddha,
> In charity
> I let a late mosquito
> Suck my blood.

ŌEMARU

> A carp dying in a tub
> Spends his last moments
> Lashing the water with his fins,
> So man wastes his short life
> In senseless agitation.

LORD MITSUTOSHI

> Minnows are helpless
> Caught in the branches of a tree
> Set out to lure them,
> So we too are tangled
> In the snare of ignorance.
>
> LORD TOSHIYORI

At Mount Asama*:

> A tenacle of bindweed
> Clinging fast
> To the hot, sunburnt
> Lava stones.

For a would-be student of *haiku:*

> Go along even with
> A thorny bush;
> Who knows but you may feel
> A gentle breeze.

In olden days the checking stations were set up for the protection of people. Now they serve only for their misery.

* Mount Asama is an active volcano. Issa must have found a bindweed growing in the devastated area of the mountain.

By the blossoming plum,
The keepers of the gate
Burn their wormwood
On people's flesh.*

Hearing a human voice
The mother deer
Took up her stand
Before her child.

The first firefly
Of the season
Slights beautifully
The pursuer's hand.

A lotus stem—
Slightly bent—
Apt emblem
Of this world.

---

* The meaning of this poem is ambiguous. All Issa says in the original is that the gatekeepers' use of moxa is getting more and more popular when the plum blossoms are in full bloom. I have translated it to emphasize the contrast between the greediness of the gatekeepers and the "innocent" plum blossoms.

> This dark space
> Under the thick leaves
> Belongs no doubt
> To our idle neighbors.

Beside the Great Pond:

> It takes but a leap
> From this swaying flower
> Of waterweed, up to
> That cloud in the sky.

There is a place in Echigo where it is said a certain person hesitated before giving the Blessed Shinran lodging for the night.*

> In Kakizaki village
> Even the cuckoo
> Stutters—
> Most hesitatingly.

---

* Shinran-Shōnin (1174–1268), founder of the Shinshū sect of Buddhism. Shinran was a disciple of Hōnen, founder of the Jōdo or Pure Land sect in the twelfth century. Shinran's teaching presented a simplified Jōdo doctrine, and the close relationship of the two sects is apparent in the common name Jōdo-Shinshū. Shinran emphasized the importance of faith and prayer *(nembutsu)* as the outward expression of faith.

Life in the great city of Edo:

> Ten cents' worth
> Of green grass
> Buys just that much wind
> In the hot weather.

> I bought
> Two cents' worth
> Of water
> To feed my lovely pink.

At Kogane-ga-hara:

> A mother horse
> Keeps watch
> While her child
> Drinks from a spring.

> What clouds tower
> In the sky
> But owe their loveliness
> To the wind.

A plague image
And a flea
Borne together
Down the river.*

Written at Morinji temple, where it is said a badger once transformed himself into an iron teakettle:

In this temple,
Once upon a time,
An iron kettle flew,
Light as a butterfly.

A mosquito bit me
Under the cherry tree,
And I spoke ill
Even of the blossoms.

This trail of ants
Surely comes all the way
From that peak of cloud
In the sky.

* Sending a plague image down the river was a popular remedy in old days. Issa refers to this custom again in Chapter Fourteen.

Chapter Eight

One day, when I was in the Forest of the Mountain God near the village of Rokugawa, in the district of Takai, I picked three small chestnuts that I later planted in a corner of my garden. One of them came up, lifting its head in the spring and beaming happily in the warm sunshine. However, it was not long after when my neighbor on the east built an addition to his house, and the plant was cut off from the light of the sun and the moon, and deprived of the benefit of rain and dew. That year it was able to grow little more than a foot in height. When winter came, they shoveled the snow from the roof according to the custom, and dumped it on the ground all around the building. It looked as if Hakusan, the Great White Mountain, had been dropped there during the night. And the narrow path that led over the top, for bringing in firewood and water, was as steep as the stone steps that climb the side of Mount Atago. As winter drew toward an end, in late February or early March, nature began to rejoice a little: fresh buds burst open in the nearby fields and early blossoms decked the trees. But this great heap of snow remained as white and deadly cold as it had been all winter. Finally the eighth of April came, when it is our custom to warn by a poem all the newborn worms in the house.* And on this day a bush warbler sang so noisily in my garden and with such knowing insistence that I went out to look for my chestnut tree, which had been buried all this time beneath the lingering snow. Alas! I found it broken at the very base by the heavy weight of snow.

Had this been a human body, we must have soon expected to see the smoke. But this old root took heart again and pushed forth two or three small leaves. By the end of the year it had become almost as high as it had been the preceding year. Yet such was the fate of this tree, that every winter the snow that fell from the roof top broke it once again, with neither pity nor regard. Seven years have passed in this way—seven cycles of frost and stars. But this poor tree has neither the strength to put forth fruits and flowers, nor the good fortune quite to die. Existence is a continuous struggle to remain simply one foot high. This can hardly be called living even for a tree.

My own life, however, does not differ greatly from

---

* Worms were a terrible nuisance in those days, and people tried to put them down by writing a frightening poem and posting it up in the house. For example,

> From the days of the gods,
> Eighth April is a good day,
> The very day whereon
> All the worms in the house
> Are put to punishment.

that of this tree. I was the first-born—the first flower to blossom—in our family, and yet I have been relegated to a place beside the late-born weeds. I have been nipped by the chill wind that blows from the slopes of the "stepmother mountain," and I have not known a single day in which I might rejoice in freedom, beneath the open sky. It is a wonder to me that the thin thread of my life has endured these fifty-seven long years—Ah, dear chestnut tree, forgive me! I had not thought of passing on to you the pattern of my own ill-fated life when I planted you inside my garden.

> Compelled to dwell
> In the sunless shade
> Of the stepmother tree,
> A pink bears a flower.

According to Buddha's teaching, there is a reason for everything that happens. If that be true, my suffering cannot be undeserved, and I may well have brought it on my own head.

> Even the magnolia
> That hangs day and night
> Above my head
> Has beautiful flowers
> In the spring.

Poems on similar themes:

All by himself,
A stepchild sleeps
On a mattress
Eked out with rushes.

                                    SŌKAN

The lonesome wind
Sent out to sweep the snow
Off the bamboo leaves—
Is he a stepchild, too?

                                    SEISHŌ

"How would I like
  To slap that fly
  On the beautiful face
  Of my stepchild.

                                    KŌSETSU

All the night
Mosquitoes bite
To make the stepchild
Weep the more.

                                    MITATSU

From the *kasen** composed in the Fourth Year of Jyōkyō [1687]:

* *Kasen* is a form of linked verse, consisting of thirty-six linked poems, though this particular *kasen* was never finished.

Once in autumn
An earnest petition untied
The rope of punishment.

The mother thereby
Winning for herself
The name and fame
Of fair stepmother.

BASHŌ

From *Gion Shūi:**

In secret
The servant buries
A beheaded body.

The stepmother
Raves aloud of her crime
In the darkness
Of the rain.

MITATSU

From the five *kasen* Bashō left in the north:**

* A critical anthology edited in 1691.
** These *kasen* have dispersed, and only fragments are known.

Covered with foliage,
He stains the grass blades
With bloody gore.

                              BASHŌ

Thus he was
Cheated of his life
Through the wiles
Of his stepmother.

                              FURYŪ

Chapter Nine

There was once a little girl who was a stepchild, and she was not allowed to eat out of a certain clay pot used for storing rice, although the rest of the children were free to help themselves. One day she heard a bush warbler crying outside the window, and she wrote:

> Warbler in the bush,
> Why do you cry?
> Is it milk you want?
> Or a clay pot?—
> Or your own mother?

**THE DAUGHTER
OF LORD TSURAYUKI**

Chapter Ten

When I was little, I kept to myself, and stayed away from the children of the village because they used to make fun of me, by singing:

> A motherless child
> Is known everywhere—
> He stands all alone
> At the front door
> And sucks his thumb
> From biting hunger.

So I used to retreat to the back yard and spend my day by the woodpile, or grieving in a dark corner. I felt so wretched that I wrote:

> Come here,
> Motherless sparrows,
> And play
> With me.

YATARŌ
Six years old

Chapter Eleven

There was once a very cruel woman who lived in the village of Tatsuta in the province of Yamato. And she refused to feed her stepchild for ten consecutive days. When the child was about to die of hunger, she showed him a bowl of rice and said, "Take this, and offer it to the stone statue that stands beside the road. If he eats it, you can have some too." There was nothing the poor child could do, except to obey. But as he sat down to pray before the stone image, a great miracle happened. The stone statue opened his gigantic mouth and devoured the rice as greedily as if he himself had been a starving child. After that, they say, the horns of cruelty dropped from the woman's brow, and she ceased discriminating between the stepchild and her own children. And if, perchance, you should ever pay a visit to this village, you can still see this same stone statue, standing where it was, and you will never fail to see fresh offerings laid before it.

> A stone image
> Before a bamboo thicket
> Savors a huge rice cake
> In the spring wind.

Chapter Twelve

Last summer, when the day for setting out bamboo slips was drawing nigh, a child was born to us. We named her Sato, hoping she might grow in wisdom, despite the fact that she was born in ignorance. This year, when her birthday came round, she bobbed her head at us, and waved her hands, and cried, which was her way of telling us she wanted a paper windmill of a kind that was then extremely popular among the small children. So we bought one for her. But she soon set to licking it and sucking it, and finally, with prodigal indifference, she flung it away. Her mind seems to flit from one thing to another, resting nowhere. Now she is busy with a clay pot, but she soon smashes it. Next she will be fascinated by a paper screen, but she soon tears it. And if we praise her for her actions, she accepts our approval at face value, and smiles delightedly. Not a cloud crosses her tiny mind. She is pure moonlight, and beams all over from head to foot, delighting us far more than the most accomplished performer on the stage could possibly do. Occasionally a visitor will ask her to point out a dog or a bird to him, and at such times she is completely captivating—from the tip of her toes to the top of her little head. She seems just like a butterfly, poised lightly on a sprig of young grass, resting her wings.

I believe this child lives in a special state of grace, and enjoys divine protection from Buddha. For when the evening comes when once a year we hold a memorial service for the dead, and I have lit the candles on the family altar, and rung the bell for prayer, she crawls out swiftly, wherever she may be, and softly folds her tiny hands, like little bracken sprouts, and says her prayers in such a sweet, small voice—in such a lovely way! For myself, I am old enough that my hair is touched with frost, and every year adds waves of wrinkles to my brow, yet so far I have not found grace with Buddha, and waste my days and months in meaningless activity. I am ashamed to think my child, who is only two years old, is closer to the truth than I. And yet no sooner do I leave the altar than I sow the seeds of future torments, hating the flies that crawl across my knees, killing the mosquitoes that swarm around the table, and even worse, drinking the wine that Buddha has prohibited.

Just as I was reproaching myself in this fashion the moonlight touched our gate, adding a breath of coolness to the evening air. A group of children dancing outside suddenly lifted their voices and cried aloud. My little girl at once threw down the little bowl she had been playing with, and crawled out to the porch, where she, too, cried out and stretched forth her hands to the moon. Watching her, I quite forgot my old age and my sinful nature, and indulged myself with the reflection that when she should be old enough to boast long hair with waving curls, we might let her dance, and that would be more beautiful, I fancied, than to hear the music of the twenty-five celestial maidens.

Not a day passes in which she gives her legs a moment's rest, at least during the daylight hours. Therefore, when night comes, she is tired out and sleeps soundly until the sun is high in the sky the following morning. Her mother takes advantage of her being in bed to do the cooking and the cleaning. When these chores are all completed, she has only a short time left to rest and catch her breath before the child wakes up. As soon as she hears the child crying in her room, she takes her up from her bed and carries her out to the yard to relieve herself. Then she nurses her. The child sucks her mother's milk with a smile on her face, and gently taps her breast to express her happiness. At this moment the mother forgets entirely all the pain she suffered in her womb and all the dirty diapers she must wash each day. She yields herself completely to the joy of having a child—a joy more precious than jewels.

> Nursing her child
> On the bed, the mother
> Counts the flea bites
> On her tiny body.

Poems on kindred themes, gathered here as playmates for this little poem on my child:

Out of the willow
A child stepped forth,
With the face
Of a monstrous ghost.

Child as he is,
He bows his head
To the sacred offerings
Of the New Year.

Asked how old he was,
A boy in a new kimono
Stretched out
All five fingers.

A poem of felicitation for a little child:

Congratulations!
Faster than our hopes
You have outgrown
Your first skirt.

A child weeping
Bids me
Pluck the full moon
From the sky.

The laughing children
Around the fire—
The only treasures
In the house.

A child arranges
Rice cakes in a row,
Each time saying
"This one is mine."

The rice cakes
For our neighbors
Weigh heavily upon
My daughter's shoulders.

All alone
Beneath a decorated tree,
A child clasps his hands
Happily at play.

I punished my child
By tying him to a tree,
Knowing a gentle breeze
Would cool him off.

Tied to a tree
In deep disgrace
The child calls out
To a firefly.

Poems on similar themes by other authors:

Both my child
And the New Year
Stood on their feet
This very morning.

                                          TEITOKU

Who knows no love
For his children
Has no wisdom to enjoy
Cherry blossoms.

                                          BASHŌ

Homage to a shrine!
Motherly affection
Helps the child
With his shoes.

                                          SHIDŌ

Once again, child,
Just once more,
Say, "flowers!"
In that little voice.

                                          RAKŌ

Between the slats
Of the window,
A tiny hand held out
To feel spring rain.

TŌRAI

A woman planting rice—
Each step brings her
Just so much closer
To her crying baby.

KISHA

A child broke off
A branch of cherry blossoms,
But how could I ever
Punish my own son?

KIKAKU

Written a hundred days after the birth of my daughter:

Bending to kiss
The soft cheek of my baby,
I hear the sharp cry
Of a shrike.

KIKAKU

Chapter Thirteen

There was once a woman who had been divorced by her husband and sent back to her parents to live. The child, however, remained with his father, and when Children's Day came around, his mother yearned to see him. But the cold eye of public disapproval prevented her, and she wrote:

> My son's banner
> Flying in the air,
> At night I come
> Just to the gate.

ANONYMOUS

I doubt whether a mother's love has even been more truly or more finely expressed. If there is anything in the world which might soften the heart of an unfeeling man it is the true affection a mother feels for her child. Had the husband heard even the faintest whisper of this poem in the wind, he must surely have called her back.

According to Buddha's teaching, man and beast are one in their essential nature. If that be true, then the mutual love between a child and his parent must be the same for animals as for men, and there can be no difference between them.

A human father
Drove away a crow
For the children
Of the sparrows.

                                  ONITSURA

For his child's sake,
A father deer
Calls out against danger
On a summer hill.

                                  GOMEI

A father frog
Stepped out,
Child on his back,
To join the chorus.

                                  TŌYŌ

A wind rustling
Through bamboo leaves
Brought a father deer
Hurrying home.

Out in the darkness
Of the passing rain,
I hear the crying
Of the childless deer.

Round the bush
That hides her children
A mother lark
Circles, singing.

Chapter Fourteen

It is a commonplace of life that the greatest pleasure issues ultimately in the greatest grief. Yet why—why is it that this child of mine, who has not tasted half the pleasures that the world has to offer, who ought, by rights, to be as fresh and green as the vigorous young needles on the everlasting pine—why must she lie here on her deathbed, swollen with blisters, caught in the loathsome clutches of the vile god of pox? Being, as I am, her father, I can scarcely bear to watch her withering away—a little more each day—like some pure, untainted blossom that is ravished by the sudden onslaught of mud and rain.

After two or three days, however, her blisters dried up and the scabs began to fall away—like a hard crust of dirt that has been softened by the melting snow. In our joy we made a boat with fresh straw, and pouring hot wine ceremoniously over it, sent it down the river with the god of smallpox on it. Yet our hopes proved all in vain. She grew weaker and weaker, and finally on the twenty-first of June, as the morning-glories were just closing their flowers, she closed her eyes forever. He mother embraced the cold body and cried bitterly. For myself—I knew well it was no use to cry, that water once flown past the bridge does not return, and blossoms that are scattered are gone beyond recall. Yet try as I would, I could not, simply could not cut the binding cord of human love.

> The world of dew
> Is the world of dew,
> And yet . . .
> And yet . . .

As I remarked above, I had left my home on the sixteenth of April, bound for the far north. However, I had journeyed no farther than Zenkōji temple, when something happened which caused me to turn back. As I reflect upon it now, I cannot help but feel it was the kindness and the consideration of the God of Travelers that brought me home.

I collected some poems on similar themes.

After the death of a child:

> If I knew a face
> Resembling my child's,
> I would go and seek it
> Among the little dancers.
>
> RAKUGO

A poem of sympathy, written for a child who lost his mother:

He sits by himself
At the dinner table
On a glorious but solitary
Autumn evening.

SHŌHAKU

On the night my daughter was buried:

Cranes cry in vain
In the dark of night,
For no blanket can ever
Cover the sod.

KIKAKU

Written on March 3—the first Girls' Day after the death of my daughter:

The dolls I wanted
To put behind me,
But out of the house,
Peach blossoms met me.*

ENSUI

* Dolls and peach blossoms are traditional decorations for Girls' Day. Hence the poet is reminded of his dead daughter both by the dolls and the peach blossoms.

Shortly after the death of my daughter:

> Night after the full moon,
> I tried in vain
> To console myself,
> Watching the wane.
>
> SAMPŪ

To a son who lost his mother:

> Why do you suck
> The handle of your fan?
> Do you still thirst
> For your mother?
>
> RAIZAN

After the death of my beloved child:

> I am stark mad
> At myself not being mad,
> Even in the midst
> Of this spring nightmare.
>
> RAIZAN

Shortly after the death of my son:

> I wonder how far
> He has wandered away
> Chasing after
> His dragonfly?
>
> CHIYO

Poems on similar themes, written by noblemen in ancient times—here set down as they occur to me:

> What a pitiful sound
> A slumbering child makes
> In the dark of the night.
> Perhaps she is dreaming
> Of her mother beside her.
>
> ANONYMOUS

> Watching an unwanted child
> Crawling after his parent,
> I cannot keep back my tears,
> For he can neither get up
> Nor face the world alone.
>
> LORD TAMEIE

> Though his mind
> Be not totally dark,
> A parent may still
> Lose his rightful way
> For love of his child.
>
> LORD KANESUKE

A passage from *Mumonkan:**

* A book of *Zen* written by Ekai, a Chinese priest of the thirteenth century.

Without lifting the foot, he arrives.
Without moving the tongue, he preaches.
Be you ever in the lead, you still must know
There is always One who comes before you.

Almost before,
At least as soon
As it is given,
I lose my fan.

Leaping a torrent
Fed by the rain,
A deer looks back
For his son.

By the fan
By accident he had left,
I learned his name
In a vast temple.

Portrait of a desperado hiding in ambush:

Murder-like,
A hungry mosquito
Sought refuge
In a ruined well.

A visit to Ōyama shrine:

> A wooden sword
> Longer than thirty feet
> Is borne aloft
> On a parade of skirts!

> Here comes a fan,
> Playful and foolish,
> Exactly like
> Torō Kaja.*

* Tarō Kaja is a famous character of the comic interlude known as *Kyōgen*.

Chapter Fifteen

Not far from the village of Murasaki someone caught a baby crow—no bigger than a lump of coal—and put it in a cage in front of his house. That night I heard the mother flying back and forth above the house, crying over and over again in the darkness. It was so pitiful, I wrote:

> Blind as the night
> For her child's love,
> A mother crow kept up
> Her pitiful moans,
> Till dawn lent her light.

Written in sympathy for a thief, captured in his own village:

> In a fitful shower,
> A bird in disgrace
> Circles the snare—
> His own village!

A poem written in sympathy for the innocent birds

who are unwittingly eating the food scattered in a tycoon's hunting ground:

> Behold, two cranes
> Eating side by side:—
> One of you is certain
> To be shot dead.

> An arrow shaft
> Takes a deadly aim
> At a mother deer
> Suckling her fawn.
>
> RISSHI

In such a case even the most ruthless hunter must yield before life's cruelty, and renounce the world.

Chapter Sixteen

My village is situated high on the gentle slope of Mount Kurohime. Therefore, no sooner has last year's snow disappeared in summer than the first frost of autumn sets in. All those trees that are not native here but have been brought in from a better climate undergo some change. For example, the mandarin shrinks to half its normal size and turns into a trifoliated orange, as is mentioned in a Chinese book.

> A common primrose
> Bears nine flowers,
> But here it fades
> With four or five.

Composed on the site of an ancient battle, where Chinzei Tametomo is said to have hurled his enemies down like stones before him:

> Hear ye, enemies!
> Viler than worms!
> Hear this cry—
> Of a cuckoo bird!*

*Here Issa has taken the words of Minamoto Tametomo (1139–1170), a seven-foot Hercules, and made them a part of his own poem. The Japanese cuckoo (*hototogisu*) is known for its extremely shrill cry.

Look how lightly
A sprig of flowering clover
Rests across
The deer's tongue.

On seeing a picture of an aged wise man standing on a rock, handing a scroll to a young man:

Long have I
Waited for thee—
To raise thy voice,
My cuckoo bird.*

A quiet life:

Still is in my house.
Still is the song
Of the cuckoo
In my silent house.

* The subject of the picture is the classical Chinese story of Kōsekikō and Chōryō. Kōsekikō, an old sage, wanted to give a secret book of strategy to young Chōryō, but every tme Chōryō came late to the appointed meeting place. Kōsekikō blamed him by saying, "Long have I waited for thee."

After slighting
The hands of man
Several times,
A firefly slips away.

"None of your tricks!"
Says a firefly
And instantly
Darts off.

Chapter Seventeen

Recently Ōritsu wrote me that Seikeishi had become a silent man.

> It matters not
> What you might say.
> Echoes will come
> From dead trees.

> A traveler stops
> At a green shade,
> To give his bleached hat
> A chance to breathe.

> "The right honorable
> Sir Frog—
> Lord of the bush—
> At your service."

> The frog looks as if
> He had just belched
> A misty cloud
> Into the sky.

A pure red leaf
Falls in glory
From the cool green
Summer shade.

With each flash
Of thunderbolt
The rice grows richer—
The world better.

How dry it looks,
The river bed
Glimpsed in the flash
Of lightning!

On the bridge—
In the evening fog—
The horse pauses
Before the hole.

Utterly helpless
In the autumn wind,
A firefly crawls away
From my hand.

During the afternoon break:

> A scarecrow
> Stands upright
> To shield a child
> From the cold wind.

On losing sight of my companion:

> In the late sun
> Of an autumn evening
> I wrote on the wall
> I had gone on first.

On July 7—at my graveyard:

> Soft *susuki* grass
> Let me sit awhile
> On thee, till at least
> I have said my prayer.

> The rat-a-tat-tat
> Of the evening drum.
> Even the woodpecker
> Stops to listen.

The woodpecker
Carefully estimates
The true value
Of my house.

In the storehouse of a temple:

The Buddha
Smiles calmly
And points his finger
At a stinkworm.*

An expert acrobat
Beautifully poised
On a single leg—
The wild goose.

On the porch
Of an old
Mountain temple—
A stag whistles.

The clear note
Of a distant stag
Teaches the hunter
To sound his horn.

---

* A worm that releases a vile smell to defend itself, like a skunk.

Talking loudly
Mushroom hunters
Descend the hill—
All empty-handed.

Beside my daughter's grave—thirty days after her death:

Here is the red flower
You wanted to pick—
Coming to bloom
In the autumn wind.

A blossom or two
Of flowering clover
Drop fluttering
From the deer's mouth.

My chrysanthemums,
What a sleep we had,
To feel so fresh
In the morning!

Tonight was made
For all idlers—
Just cool enough
For rambling.

A little child
Picked with his fingers
A drop of dew—
And lo, it vanished!

Chapter Eighteen

"Seek your shelter beneath the largest tree." And indeed there are always some who are ready to kneel down before the wealthy or to oil their tongues in the presence of the powerful.

Here in this village is a large chestnut tree that stands near Suwa shrine. And although the tree does not seem particularly heavy laden, not a person comes by who cannot pick up a chestnut or two every morning.

Chapter Nineteen

I saw the full moon at Nashimoto's house in the village of Takaino.

> Alone at home
> My wife is surely
> Gazing at the moon,
> Like myself.

I saw a total eclipse of the moon. It began at ten o'clock, reaching its climax at midnight, and coming to an end at two in the morning.

> Such is man,
> The moon viewers
> Dwindle faster than
> The moon in eclipse.

> The world of man
> Being what it is,
> Even the full moon
> Must suffer eclipse.

> Playing smart,
> Many a man and woman
> Presume to discuss
> The moon's eclipse.

> When the cups
> Are empty,
> We sit down at last
> To see the moon.

No one knows the smell of one's own bean paste:

> The village bumpkins
> Sing the praise of their
> "Buckwheat country"
> Beneath the full moon.*

On September 16 — at a chrysanthemum-viewing party at my friend Shōfūin's house:

> Like an old god
> Of Harvest, my host
> Leans upon his hoe—
> Amid chrysanthemums.

---

* Issa's country is known as "buckwheat country" because a great quantity of buckwheat is produced and consumed there.

We had a walk
Through the garden
Of chrysanthemums,
Wine cups in our hands.

Our host lectures
On his chrysanthemums
Using his stick,
Like a wandering priest.

A huge, bold man
Labors in the garden
Amid chrysanthemums,
A towel about his head.

The chrysanthemums
Are wonderful,
But unfortunately
Our host does not drink.

I dreamed of the smiling face of my daughter:

Only in the dream
My daughter takes
A ripe musk melon
Up to her soft cheek.

Driven away by men,
The migrating birds
Follow their course
Through this village.

Through twigs and leaves,
As through hoops,
A swarm of titmice leap,
Flaunting their tricks.

The shrike screams
From the top of his tree.
His stock of patience
Must have run out.

A skinny mantis,
Less than an inch long,
Bravely battled—
Body and soul together.

Standing on a hill in the village of Takaino:

In the autumn wind,
The compass points
Of its own accord
To my village home.

The village women
Wash their clothes
By a lamp hanging
From a pine tree.

My wild geese,
Stay with me.
No matter where you go,
The same autumn evening.

Advice to a young priest—I wrote it on his fan:

Look upon thy shadow
And be ashamed—
Rambling thus
On a cold night!

The migrating birds
Pass above my village,
No doubt saying to us,
"To hell with you!"

HAKUHI

In the green shade,
A wineshop opens,
And sells the product
Of the fresh harvest.

SHIEI

Peaceful old age—a dream:

> In my secret heart
> I give thanks
> To my children
> On a frosty night.

> A cricket hops
> Like a shadow
> In the golden dust
> Of the winnower.

> Were you smaller,
> My chrysanthemum,
> Would you be fettered
> In deep disgrace?

When I am utterly lost:

> Through the cold
> Nighttime air
> A horse bays to lead me
> To a shit-house.

Do not fight,
But help one another
On your way—
Dear migrating birds.

Standing close together,
Stags are licking
The first frost and ice
Off one another's coats.

"Wolf dung!"
At these words
A cold shiver runs
Through my body.

Golden maple leaves
In their prime—
Here used to scrape
A wine barrel.

At the slightest
Movement of my lips,
A thousand plovers
Rise as one.

Crackling charcoal
And a loud cough
Promise a good day
In the early morning.

The drip-drop
Of autumn rain—
Even the bath boy slacks
The beat of his drum.

Cold blast of wind—
A blind masseur
Fancied he had heard
A distant voice calling.

On seeing a beggar in front of Zenkōji temple:

A beggar sitting
In the evening rain.
Before him—a box—
And a few coins.

By his own momentum
A boy toppled over
Backwards—
A radish in his hand.

Pure and white—
The first snow of the year
Lies all alone
Behind the house.

A servant hurries home
Along the Frost Bridge*
In the biting teeth
Of a stormy wind.

After the sermon,
The farmer is so kind
As to let me walk
Through his field.

A few flakes of snow
From the sky of Shinano—
I cannot think
Of a single joke.

An old duffer, if you like,
But yet no criminal—
Still am I confined
Within this cold prison.

* It is believed that a bridge with this name (Samusa Bashi) once existed in Tsukiji, downtown Tōkyō.

Because there are burglars haunting the town:

    My house is invaded
    And completely taken
    By noisy watchmen
    On a frosty night.

    Whatever we say
    About snowmen,
    It is as short-lived
    As snowmen themselves.

    An old housewife
    Proudly demonstrates
    The proper cutting
    Of the rice cake.

    The helpers arrived,
    So the children report
    Pounding of the rice cakes
    Has begun next door.

The New Year is coming:

> Don't gripe!
> It is about the time
> Rice-cake flowers bloom
> On the willow tree.*

> When begging actors
> Come dancing along,
> Grownups beat children
> In merrymaking.

On my way to Edo:

> I am an easy prey
> Of cold criticism.
> "Starling" I am called
> Along the post road.**

* A few days before New Year's everyone is engaged in making rice cakes *(mochi)* and adorning their homes with rice-cake flowers. The eating of these rice cakes is the great feature of the New Year's Day celebration.

** During winter months, many people from Issa's district went to Tōkyō as seasonal workers, and these people were nicknamed "starlings" because they formed swarms along the road.

At Gojiinga-hara:

> A cheap-looking house
> Of the cheapest harlot
> Stands shivering
> In the wintery blast.

At Ryōgoku bridge:

> At the midwinter
> Purification,
> Tattooed dragons crawl
> Along men's backs.

I have heard tales of a certain man who resolved that once he had retired to the further side of the Kamo River, he would never cross it again. But I, in my weakness, have deserted the mountain that was once my refuge, and exposing my white hairs to the wind, return once more to see this land of fame and wealth.

> I am ashamed to add
> Another year to my age,
> Returning thus
> To the city of Edo.

"In with the luck!
 Out with the demon!"
And then for a while
Just children's voices.*

Left to themselves, people take to evil ways:

> My winter confinement
> Has taught me to eat
> Rare and strange things
> Of all kinds!

December 21—spring begins today according to the calendar:

> On this day
> A single cry of our throat
> Is said to drive away
> The demons.

* On the eve of spring, people throw beans at demons, crying, "In with the luck, out with the demon." Children are particularly fond of the celebration. According to the old lunar calendar then in use spring sometimes came befor the first of January.

> Whatever green
> The wheat may gain
> Is from today
> Earnings of the New Year.

People return their talismans to the nearest shrine at the end of the year:

> A budding plum tree
> Bends to the earth
> Like an old man—
> With a box of talismans.

Chapter Twenty

On December 27—a fine day:
My wife rose early in the morning and prepared a hot breakfast. As this was the day on which our neighbor, Sonoemon, customarily made his rice cakes, we expected he might send us some fresh baked, as he had in former years. If he should, we thought, we might as well have them with our usual breakfast while they were still warm. We waited and waited, but alas —the cakes did not come. When we finally decided to eat—our breakfast had grown cold.

>Just seemingly
>Our neighbor's rice cakes
>Came to my gate
>As in former years.

Chapter Twenty-one

Those who insist on salvation by faith and devote their minds to nothing else, are bound all the more firmly by their singlemindedness, and fall into the hell of attachment to their own salvation. Again, those who are passive and stand to one side waiting to be saved, consider that they are already perfect and rely rather on Buddha than on themselves to purify their hearts—these, too, have failed to find the secret of genuine salvation. The question then remains—how do we find it? But the answer, fortunately, is not difficult.

We should do far better to put this vexing problem of salvation out of our minds altogether and place our reliance neither on faith nor on personal virtue, but surrender ourselves completely to the will of Buddha. Let him do as he will with us—be it to carry us to heaven, or to hell. Herein lies the secret.

Once we have determined on this course, we need care nothing for ourselves. We need no longer ape the busy spider by stretching the web of our desire across the earth, nor emulate the greedy farmer by taking extra water into our own fields at the expense of our neighbors. Moreover, since our minds will be at peace, we need not always be saying our prayers with hollow voice, for we shall be entirely under the benevolent direction of Buddha.

This is the salvation—this the peace of mind we teach in our religion. Blessed be the name of Buddha.

> Trusting to Buddha
> Good and bad,
> I bid farewell
> To the departing year.

Written on this twenty-ninth day of December, in the Second Year of Bunsei [1819], at the age of fifty-seven.

THE END

Postscript 1

This book was written by Issa, priest of Haikaiji temple, in Shinano, and though it seems to be written very casually, it is in reality a thick and flourishing grove of poetry. Not a single poem in this book is intended merely for a joke. All in some way touch the high and holy world of priests and temples. The style employed in this work is Issa's own. It is not an imitation of Kenkō, Ikkyū, or Hakuin. And yet Issa follows faithfully Bashō's principle of *hosomi* (slenderness). He intentionally keeps one foot planted in the dust of the world, and the range of his human sympathies is far greater than can adequately be described. Indeed, what more need be said?

> On the day of the Spring Equinox
> In the Fourth Year of Kaei [1851]
> Hyōkai Shisanjin

Cherry blossoms
Are likewise in full bloom
On the other shore
Of the life's stream.

Postscript II

The priest Izen was a great eccentric in the days of Genroku. The priest Issa is a great eccentric of recent times. The comic humor of his verse is known to everyone. Yet his poetry is comic only on the surface:—it is serious at heart. This book has long been treasured in the house of Isshi of Nakano village. It is indeed a strange mixture of sobriety and jest—of tragedy and comedy—and it contains all kinds of human passions and conditions, thoughts and meditations. Had this been written a hundred and sixty years ago, what would Bashō have said of it? Would he have called Issa an elder or a younger brother of the priest Izen?

[Undated]

SEIAN SAIBA

www.ingramcontent.com/pod-product-compliance
Lightning Source LLC
Chambersburg PA
CBHW021712230426
43668CB00008B/807